Eliot Weinberger | Wildlife

Eliot Weinberger

GIRAMONDO

Wildlife

First published 2012
from the Writing & Society Research Centre
at the University of Western Sydney
by the Giramondo Publishing Company
PO Box 752 Artarmon NSW 1570 Australia
www.giramondopublishing.com

Designed by Harry Williamson
Typeset by Andrew Davies
in 10/14.5 pt Minion Pro
Printed and bound by Ligare Book Printers
Distributed in Australia by NewSouth Books

National Library of Australia
Cataloguing-in-Publication entry:

Weinberger, Eliot
Wildlife / Eliot Weinberger
ISBN: 9781920882839 (pbk.)
814.54

These essays are taken or adapted from the books *Works on Paper* (1986), *Outside Stories* (1992), *Karmic Traces* (2000) and *An Elemental Thing* (2007), all published by New Directions. Four of the essays are previously unpublished in book form.

"Han Yu's Address to the Crocodiles", and "Paper Tigers" from *Works on Paper*, reprinted by permission of New Directions Publishing Corp.

Contents

The Creation

On June 9, 1603, Samuel de Champlain attended an Algonquin victory ceremony along the banks of the Ottawa River. He sat with the Grand Sagamore, Besouat, in front of a row of spikes topped with the heads of the defeated enemy, and watched as the Grand Sagamore's wives and daughters danced before them entirely naked, wearing only necklaces of dyed porcupine quills.

After the dancing, the conversation turned to theology. The Grand Sagamore told Champlain that there was one sole God. After God had created all things, he stuck some arrows in the ground, and these turned into the men and women who populated the earth.

Champlain told the Grand Sagamore that this was pagan superstition and false. There was indeed one sole God, but after He had created all things, he took a lump of clay and made a man, and then took one of the man's ribs and made a woman. The Grand Sagamore looked doubtful, but following the rules of hospitality, remained silent.

Naked Mole-Rats

Naked mole-rats have no fur, but their lips are hairy. Their pinkish mottled skin is loose and hangs in folds, like something that has lost a great deal of weight, the easier to squirm through their narrow tunnels. Incisors protrude from their mouths like pincers, the only feature of their undefined faces. One naked mole-rat can fit across your fingers, its tail dangling down. They have been under the earth for at least three million years.

They never surface. They are blind. Their world is not a labyrinth, but a straight tunnel, a mile or two long, with innumerable cul-de-sacs branching off, and certain larger chambers. They live on the tuberous roots that grow towards them.

As many as three hundred inhabit a colony, moving a ton of dirt every month. They have a caste system, tripartite like the Indian. The smallest among them are the diggers and food-gatherers who work through the night in a line, male and female equally, the first gnawing the earth and kicking it back to the next, who kicks it back, until the last, who digs a temporary hole to the surface, kicks out the dirt, its rump exposed to the moon and predators, and then plugs the hole again. When they come across a root, they chew off pieces to carry to the others.

The medium-sized are the warriors, who try to fend off the rufous-beaked snakes, the file snakes, the white-lipped snakes, and the sand boas that sometimes find their way in. They attack with repeated tiny bites that are, if the snake is small enough, mysteriously instantly fatal. When, by chance, two colonies of naked mole-rats tunnel into each other, their warriors fight to the death.

These castes serve the largest, who are the breeders. Unique among mammals, only one female reproduces. She is by far the longest and the fattest and the most aggressive in the colony. If she dies there is chaos. She is attended by one to three males, who do nothing else. They spend their time nuzzling her; have sex, initiated by her, by mounting her from behind for fifteen seconds, bracing themselves by holding their front legs against the walls of the tunnel, and mainly failing. When she becomes pregnant, the teats of every colony member, male and female, enlarge, reach their peak at the birth, and then shrink. Just before birth, the female runs wildly through the tunnels.

She has four or five litters a year of a dozen pups. The babies have transparent skin through which their internal organs are clearly visible. Only a few survive, and they live long lives, twenty years or more. The dead babies are eaten, except for their heads. At times the live ones are eaten too.

Interbred so long, they are virtually clones. One dead-end branch of the tunnel is their toilet: they wallow there in the soaked earth so that all will smell alike. They are nearly always touching each other, rubbing noses, pawing, nuzzling. When their tunnel is blocked they work from both sides and reconnect it perfectly. They sleep in a packed heap in the nesting chamber, with the breeders on the top, staying warm, each naked mole-rat with its nose pressed against the anus and genitals of another.

They are continually cruel in small ways, clanking teeth, breathing rapidly into each other's open mouths, batting, swiping, biting, pulling one another's baggy skin, shoving each other sometimes a yard down the tunnel. But only the females who compete for the role of breeder inflict real harm. Wounded, the defeated female crouches shivering in the toilet, ignored by the others until she dies.

The tunnels are never silent. Naked mole-rats make at least seventeen sounds: soft chirps and loud chirps, high-pitched and low, tooth-grinding, trills, twitters, tongue-taps, sneezes, screams, hisses, grunts. Different sounds for when they bump into each other, when they piss, when they mate, when they're disturbed, alarmed, wounded, when they shove each other, when they meet a foreigner such as a beetle, when they find food, when they can't find food.

They clean their feet with their teeth. They clean their teeth with their feet. They yawn. They shiver. They scratch themselves after they piss. They bask near the surface, in the warm sunless earth. They doze with their short legs splayed, their huge heads drooping. They double over, mouth to anus, to eat their own shit.

They scurry with eyes closed, forward or backward at the same speed, over and under each other. They change direction by somersaulting. They find their way, when they don't know it, by darting forward till their nose bumps the wall, dart backwards, adjust the angle, dart forward again. Sometimes a naked mole-rat will suddenly stop, stand on its hind-legs, and remain motionless, its head pressed against the roof of the tunnel. Above its head is the civil war in Somalia. Their hearing is acute.

Certain Changs

Chang Chih-ho, in the 8th century, lost his post under the Emperor and retreated to the mountains. He devoted himself to fishing, but never used any bait, for his object was not to catch fish.

It was recorded in the 12th century, in the *Collected Stories of Anomalies*, that Chang T'ien-hsi dreamed that a green dog with a long body came from the south and tried to bite him.

Chang Seng-yu, in the 6th century, painted a pair of dragons without eyes on the Temple of Peace and Joy, and warned that the painting should never be completed. A skeptic filled in the eyes, and the walls of the temple crashed to ruins as the dragons flew off.

It was recorded in the 10th century, in the *Old History of the T'ang Dynasty*, that Chang Chih-ho's mother became pregnant when she dreamed that a maple tree was growing from her stomach, that Chang Yueh's mother became pregnant when she dreamed that a jade swallow flew in from the southwest and entered her body, and that Chang

Chiu-ling's mother became pregnant when she dreamed that nine cranes came down from the sky and gathered in the courtyard of her house. It was noted that the boy was named Chiu-ling, which means "nine extra years."

Chang Chu, a poet in the 13th century, wrote a line, "The cataclysm of red sheep," that no one has ever been able to explain.

Chang Hsu-ching, a Taoist, no one remembers exactly when, obtained the elixir of life and discovered that tigers would do his bidding.

Chang Ch'ao, in the 17th century, said: "Flowers must have butterflies, mountains must have streams, rocks must have moss, the ocean must have seaweed, old trees must have creepers, and people must have obsessions."

It was recorded in the 12th century, in *The Valley Embroidered with Myriad Flowers*, that Lady Chang dreamed that a Taoist priest named Mountain Dweller with a Heart of Jade appeared to her and asked her help with his rebirth. Soon after, she gave birth to a crane. The family was alarmed and threw the chick into the river. It was recorded that Lady Chang's uncle intervened: "I have heard that the births of extraordinary men who appear between long intervals are always unusual." The family rushed to the river and found a child covered with feathers. It was noted that, a month later, the feathers fell off.

Chang Jung, a poet in the 5th century, was given a fan made of white egret feathers by a Taoist priest, who told him that strange things should be given to strange people. The Emperor said that the kingdom couldn't stand to be without one man like Chang Jung and couldn't stand to be with two.

Both Chang Cho in the 8th century and Chang Chiu-ko in the 11th century could cut out paper butterflies that would flutter around and then return to their hands.

It was recorded in the 8th century, in the *Collected Records of Court and Countryside*, that Chang Cho dreamed that he was wearing a crimson robe and riding a donkey. He could not understand why, wearing the robes of a minister, he was not riding a horse.

Chang Huang-yen, the last supporter of the Ming Dynasty in the 17th century, retreated to a barren island, where he trained apes to warn him of an enemy approach.

Chang Hua, in the 3rd century, wrote a famous rhapsody or rhymed prose poem (*fu*) on the wren: The wren is a tiny bird. It eats only a few grains; it makes its nest on a single branch; it can only fly a few feet; it takes up little space and does no harm. Its feathers are drab; it is useless to humankind, but it too receives the force of life. Ducks and geese can fly up to the clouds, yet they are shot down with arrows, for their flesh is plump. Kingfishers and peacocks must die because their feathers are beautiful. The falcon is fierce, but is kept on a tether; the parrot is intelligent, but is locked in a cage, where it is forced to repeat its master's words. Only the little wren, worthless and unlovely, is free.

Wrens

Wrens live almost everywhere; they eat almost anything; they adapt to most climates – converting, for example, from polygamy to monogamy where food is scarce. There are twenty million of them in the British Isles alone. They build their nests almost anywhere, even in the beard of Edward Lear's Old Man With a Beard. The pastor-naturalist Rev. Edward A. Armstrong wrote that he found a nest in a human skull, but he didn't explain how.

Yet the prolific and anonymous wren is not simple. In many of the European languages, its name means "king of the birds" or "winter king." Killing one was bad luck: you'd break a bone, break out in pimples, get struck by lightning; the fingers on the hand that did the deed would shrivel and drop off; your cows would have blood in their milk.

Once a year, an exception was made. In most of France, Ireland, and the British Isles, there was a ritualised wren hunt that is recorded in Medieval texts, is undoubtedly much older, and was widespread until recent times. Though it varied from village to village, the essential ceremony was the same:

Sometime around the winter solstice – on Christmas or St. Stephen's Day (December 26) or New Year's Eve or New Year's Day or

Twelfth Night – boys or young men would blacken their faces and dress up in crazy clothes – women's dresses or pyjamas or suits of straw – and, accompanied by fife and drums, would go out to beat the bushes for a wren. The boy who successfully caught one was named King of the Hunt and often required to perform tasks such as jumping naked in a lake. The slain wren was hung on a pole with its wings outstretched or carried on a bier decorated with ribbons and mistletoe or even in a miniature house complete with doors and windows. Its size was exaggerated: the boys pretended to stagger under the weight of the pole or bier, and in some places the bird was bound with heavy ropes and placed in a cart pulled by four oxen.

The Wren Boys then proceeded from house to house, singing songs and collecting coins. One of the versions of the song went:

The wren, the wren, the king of all birds,
St. Stephen's Day was caught in the furze;
Although he is little, his family's great,
I pray you, good landlady, give us a treat.

The money paid for a banquet and a dance that night, one that usually featured transgressive games or rituals for the newly wedded and the still unmarried. The next morning the wren was solemnly buried.

That the little wren comes from somewhere far in the past is evident in the stories about it. The wren is a subverter of Christianity. As St. Stephen was about to escape from jail, a wren landed on the guard's face and woke him up, leading to the saint's martyrdom. The Irish St. Moling cursed all wrens because one ate his pet fly "that used to be making music for me." St. Malo chose to freeze rather than wear his cloak, for a wren had built a nest in it. Wrens are sometimes known as the "bird magician" or the "Druid bird."

The wren, in countless stories, is the enemy of the eagle, whom it usually outwits. The soaring eagle is the quintessential symbol of the sky, storms, and the sun. The wren – which doesn't fly high, which creeps into mouse-holes and crevices – is an emblem of the earth. (In Greece, Trochilos the wren was the son of Triptolemos, the inventor of the plow.) And more: through the gender reversal so common in folklore, the wren, though "king of the birds," is female. She is Jenny Wren or Kitty Wren, the wife of Cock Robin, the universal bringer of fire. The wren is pagan, chthonic, female.

Four to six thousand years ago in these same parts, two distinct kinds of megaliths were constructed: circular passage graves with a single entrance and rectangular gallery graves with two entrances. As each is confined to various large and specific geographical areas, and as they rarely overlap, it is believed that they represent two distinct cultures or religions.

In the 1950s, the Reverend Armstrong mapped all the places

where the Wren Hunt occurred and discovered that it was largely absent from the areas where gallery graves are found. In Ireland, the area of passage graves and Wren Boys and the area of gallery graves and no Wren Boys corresponded almost exactly with the national entities now known as Ireland and Northern Ireland. Wrens go deep.

Flies

A fly on a window cannot understand how there is a world he sees but cannot reach. A fly, as it has often been said, on a piece of shit is in paradise; a fly in honey is doomed. Vishnu's fly whisk, made of yak hair, signifies the dharma: they are and we are and we cannot help but flick them away. A fly knows a pleasure denied to mammals: mating in mid-air. Beelzebub, the Lord of the Flies. A man who saw like a fly – kaleidoscopically – would go mad; a fly who saw like a man would be depressed by linearity. Apollonius of Tyana rid Byzantium of flies by making a bronze fly and burying it under a pillar. A fly may be thinking of other things, or not thinking; it doesn't look where it's going, and crashes into a screen. Yoko Ono filmed a fly climbing a breast like the conquest of Everest. Russians girls used to carve turnips into coffins and bury flies. The fly on the man's open wound was merely being a fly, enjoying the fact that the man was merely human. Charles Reznikoff, given a job in Hollywood with nothing to do, wrote poems about silence and solitude to the flies on his desk.

A child dreams of himself in the first version of the movie *The Fly*: the tiny human head on the fly's body, trapped in a web, squeaking

"Help me." An adult dreams of himself in the second version of the movie *The Fly*: she still loves him no matter how monstrous he has become.

A Donkey in Kweichow

According to the T'ang poet Liu Tsung-yüan, there were no donkeys in Kweichow, until a man, "fond of curiosities," brought one in on a boat. He soon found the donkey useless, and let it loose in the hills.

A tiger came across the donkey and, because of its enormous size, mistook it for a god. When the donkey brayed, the tiger's heart turned weak. Nevertheless, the tiger kept watching the donkey. He tentatively circled closer, then closer, and finally brushed against the donkey's side. The donkey kicked out in annoyance.

The donkey had revealed what it was. The tiger roared, leaped, and ripped open its throat.

Political Analysts in Medieval India

In medieval India, one of the best sources for reliable political commentary, as well as informed speculation on the future, was a dog. The practice was widespread for centuries, but the most detailed surviving description of it comes from an encyclopedia compiled in 1363 by a certain Shārngadhara, a Brahmin functionary in the desert kingdom of Mewar, now part of Rajasthan, and recently translated in part by the Indologist David Gordon White. Shārngadhara advises us that "in answer to the question What is happening in the world?, a mortal may place his entire trust" in five creatures: the fawn, the spotted owl, the crow, the female jackal, and the dog. Like any other roundtable of commentators, however, not all of these were equally persuasive. In fact, "The first four are, by their nature, barely intelligible. The dog is far easier to understand."

Of course, not merely any dog could become a political analyst. It had to be young, healthy, without defects and, above all, entirely black, presumably to ensure that its opinions were consistent and unwavering, not mottled with qualifications or doubt. Working as it did in a royalist milieu, its tail, naturally, could not "bend to the left."

In appreciation from its grateful public, the opining dog was ritually bathed at sundown, and given a feast of milk and special cakes made in the shape of dogs: a practice that was refreshingly candid about the dog-eat-dog nature of politics. It was then placed in its forum, a multicoloured mandala painted on the ground, and – this being India – was honoured at exceeding length with songs, prayers, incense, lamps, flowers, food, and ritual fires. At dawn, having undoubtedly dozed through such welcoming remarks, the dog was ready to impart its expertise.

Generally speaking, things were going quite well in the kingdom if the dog scratched its head with its right forepaw, scratched its left paw with its right paw, scratched its right ear with its right paw, urinated with its right hind leg raised or, if female, scratched its belly. There were grave problems with the government if the dog yawned, vomited, ran away, hiccupped, coughed, seemed anxious, fell asleep and shook violently, dug a hole, howled, or looked into the sun.

As a kingdom's fate is largely dependent on the members of its royal family, the dog was especially valued for its insights into the inner palace. Its bark could indicate whether any acts committed by the king in a previous life would have consequences in the present day. The manner in which it urinated was a discussion of dynastic continuity: whether the pregnant queen would give birth to a son or daughter, or miscarry. If the dog lay down without scratching itself, someone in the royal household was gravely ill. The dog also knew who would live to old age, who would soon die, what important emissaries were on the way, whether the queen had a lover, and even whether the lover was someone within the palace or an outsider. In perhaps its most arcane form of commentary, a female dog could reveal that the king's enemies were plotting against him at that very moment by attempting to have sex – Shārngadhara does not explain how – with a young bull at a crossroads.

Like many strident editorialists, the dog tended to urge courses of action which would not directly affect it. For example: "A dog may encourage a king to go into battle." This was not, however, uninformed jingoism. The dog was equally an expert on military strength: "When two armies are locked in battle, it can tell which will win the undisputed victory, which will deal the crushing blow." Canine analysis was particularly useful in times of hostility between two kingdoms: If the dog faced east, there would be war. If it walked east, the war would be followed by a reconciliation. If it walked both east and west, there would be continued hostility, but no actual fighting. If it perked up its ears and barked at the sun, peace was at hand.

Our political analysts pride themselves as "insiders"; in India, the dog was valued because it was so far removed from the corridors of power, even from the norms of life. The Indian dog is the consummate outsider: It stays awake at night, watching, and sleeps in the day. It can be man's "best friend" or turn suddenly rabid. Contrary to the dietary laws, it eats anything. (A common name for dogs in India was "vomit-eater.")

Transgressing the restrictions of caste, it has sex indiscriminately with any other dog, and thus is itself the product of miscegenation, a sign of the lowest castes. And it frequently inhabits the cremation grounds, the nowhere land between life and death, where it feeds on carrion.

In India, the dog was trusted and prized for its opinions precisely because of its independence. It was tied to no leash, and it never had lunch with the king.

Belize

Flung flying down the unpaved and cratered Hummingbird Highway, past the village of Hummingbird, ten houses on stilts. The Hummingbird River flows down from the Hummingbird Mountains, each one of which is called Mt. Hummingbird. It is said the people here have exceptionally small imaginations. They say a woman is as beautiful as a hummingbird, a boy is as quick as a hummingbird, a remark as sharp as a hummingbird's beak, the morning as hazy as hummingbirds' wings, a man as silent as a hummingbird, things are as small as or larger than hummingbirds, and the food is so good a hummingbird might hover over the plate. When a man dies, he is born again as a hummingbird. When a hummingbird dies, it goes to paradise. There it lives forever in the village of Hummingbird, by the Hummingbird River, under the Hummingbird Mountains. Everything is the same, except that there is no Hummingbird Highway, for there's no place else to go.

Paper Tigers

The Maharajah of Rewa, according to his English Adviser, had his own method of hunting tiger:

He found the easiest way to bag tigers was to take with him a book and a monkey on a long string. When seated in the *machan* [a platform in the trees] he would release the monkey, who immediately climbed into the top branches. He would then give the signal for the beat to start and settle down to read. As soon as the tiger approached the monkey would spot him and give the cough with which all monkeys warn the jungle folk that "Sher Khan" the tiger is on the prowl. His Highness would then quickly put down his book and pick up the rifle.

At the turning of a page, the apparition of a tiger:

Berggasse 19, March 10, 1933: H.D., one of the last patients of Freud, records her sessions with the Professor:

Curiously in fantasy I think of a tiger. Myself as a tiger? This tiger may pounce out. Suppose it should attack the frail and delicate old Professor? Do I fear my own terrors of the present situation, the lurking "beast" may or may not destroy him? I mention this tiger as a past nursery fantasy. Suppose it should actually materialise? The Professor says, "I have my protector." He indicates Yofi, the little lioness curled at his feet.

And a few days later:

I spoke again of our toy animals and he reminded me of my tiger fantasy. Wasn't there a story, "the woman and the tiger," he asked. I remembered "The Lady or the Tiger."

A King invents a peculiar system of justice: The accused is placed in a large arena before the entire populace and must open one of two identical doors. Behind one, a tiger, which will leap out and tear the man to pieces, establishing his guilt. Behind the other, a lady "most suitable to his years and station," whom he must immediately marry as a reward for his innocence. ("It mattered not that he might already possess a wife and family, or that his affections might be engaged upon an object of his own selection. The King allowed no such subordinate arrangements to interfere with his great scheme of retribution and reward.") The accused, then, must "open either [door] he pleased, without having the slightest idea whether, in the next instant, he was to be devoured or married."

As might be expected, the King has a daughter, and she falls in love with a handsome commoner. Learning of this transgression, the King declares that the boy must be sent to the arena. For one door, the most ferocious tiger in the land is found; for the other, the most beautiful maiden – more beautiful, in fact, than the King's own daughter.

Before the trial, the wily daughter discovers the secret of the doors, and as the boy enters the arena she signals him with her right hand. He immediately opens the right door...But which would be worse for this "hot-blooded semi-barbaric princess": to see her beloved ripped to shreds, or happily married to a woman more lovely than she? What was the meaning of her sign? Or, as the story ends: "Which came out of the opened door – the lady, or the tiger?"

Frank Stockton's "The Lady, or the Tiger?," first published in *The Century Magazine* in 1882, quickly became an international obsession. At the time inconclusive endings were vexatious, not modern, and for the twenty years until his death Stockton was besieged with solutions, sequels and threats. Among the latter, Rudyard Kipling subjected Stockton to a bit of impeccable Raj ragging, as reported by the San Francisco *Wave* in 1896:

Stockton and Kipling met at an author's reception, and after some preliminary talk, the former remarked: "By the way, Kipling, I'm thinking of going over to India some day myself." "Do so, my dear fellow," replied Mr. Kipling, with suspicious warmth of cordiality. "Come as soon as ever you can! And, by the way, do you know what we'll do when we get you out there, away from your friends and family? Well, the first thing will be to lure you out into the jungle and have you seized and bound by our trusty wallahs. Then we'll lay you on your back and have one of our very biggest elephants stand over you and poise his ample forefoot directly over your head. Then I'll say in my most insinuating tones, 'Come now, Stockton, which was it – The Lady or the Tiger?'…"

And Mrs. Stockton recorded this scene in her diary:

Miss Evans, our niece, wrote to us that a missionary who was visiting her mission station among the Karens [a tribe in northeast Burma], told her she had just come from a distant wild tribe of Karens occasionally visited by missionaries and to her surprise was immediately asked by them if she knew who came out the door, The Lady or the Tiger? Her explanation of it was that some former visitor had read to them this story as suited to their fancy; and as she had just come from the outside world they supposed she could tell the end of it.

Men generally favored the lady, women the tiger. An exception was Robert Browning, who declared he had "no hesitation in supposing that such a princess, under such circumstances, would direct her lover to the tiger's door." In fact, Freud's slip was to the point: it is an *and*, not an *or*, proposition. The choice between lady or tiger, "devoured or married," was to its readers hardly a choice at all. As one W.S. Hopson of San Francisco wrote in 1895:

When my wife flies into a passion,
And her anger waxes wroth,
I think of the Lady and the Tiger,
And sigh that I chose them both.

A few years after Stockton's death, Elinor Glyn's *Three Weeks* (1907) was the steamy bestseller of its day, its success due largely to its famous seduction scene on a tiger-skin rug:

Paul entered from the terrace. And the loveliest sight of all, in front of the fire, stretched at full length, was his tiger and on him – also at full length – reclined the lady…

"No! You mustn't come near me, Paul…Not yet. You brought me the tiger. Ah that was good! My beautiful tiger!" And she gave a movement like a snake, of joy to feel its fur under her, while she stretched out her hands and caressed the creature where the hair turned white and black at the side, and was deep and soft.

"Beautiful one! Beautiful one!" she purred. "And I know all your feelings and your passions, and now I have got your skin – for the joy of my skin." And she quivered again with a movement of a snake.

Alas, tiger's fur is short and coarse, and would make for an itchy tryst. But Glyn's book effectively played on the fusion of lady and tiger in the popular imagination. It also inspired this piece of anonymous doggerel (and mnemonic guide to proper pronunciation):

Would you like to sin
with Elinor Glyn
on a tiger skin?
Or would you prefer
to err
with her
on some other fur?

Tiger, woman, passion. Glyn's sin comes out of ancient tradition, for the tiger has always been first female, and later male.

The earliest recorded tigers in the West were those presented to Seleuces I (312–280 B.C.E.). (Alexander of course had seen tigers in Persia.) In Latin poetry *tigris* is always feminine (the word means "arrow," and was applied to the swiftness of the animal and the river); in Roman art tigresses are nearly always portrayed. Female tiger is often paired with male lion, much as Freud's "lioness" Yofi checks H.D.'s tiger. Bacchus' chariot was drawn by such a pair. It is a distinction Keats articulates in "Hyperion" as "tiger-passioned, lion-thoughted." (As, shifting species, the Brontës' cat was named "Tiger," their dog "Keeper.") As late as the 18th century it was believed that the way to capture a tiger cub – the only way to get a tiger for one's menagerie – was the procedure first described by Claudian nearly two thousand years before: steal the cub and, with the tiger in pursuit, scatter mirrors in her path; her female vanity is such that she will gaze fondly in the mirror and forget about the baby.

In China the tiger was originally *yin*: associated with the underworld, and with the West (where the sun enters the underworld). In the *feng-shui* system of geomancy, it is paired with the *yang* green dragon. (The Buddhists would later reverse the genders of the tiger/green dragon pair – stressing the tiger's *yang* nobility, and pointing out, quite correctly, that tigers wear the character for "king," *wang* 王 on their foreheads.) Wordsworth's description in *The Prelude* of Jacobin Paris as "Defenceless as a wood where tigers roam" may owe something to

Virgil's characterisation of Rome as "a wilderness of tigers." But both are identical to the stock Chinese metaphor for a corrupt and sick society: a tiger (*yin*) in a bamboo grove (*yang*), the dark within the light.

The Chinese tiger-monster, the *t'ao t'ieh* ("the glutton") is prominent as early as the Shang dynasty. The *t'ao t'ieh* is a devourer, and almost always appears in funerary art; sometimes the burial urn itself is in the shape of a tiger. It is the earth eating the dead to provide nourishment for the living – much as the Greek word *sarcophagus* means "to eat flesh." (In the pre-Columbian Americas where there were no tigers, the jaguar was its exact equivalent: an earth-image paired in Mesoamerica with the sky-symbol of the feathered serpent, in South America commonly portrayed in burial urns. The whole city of Cuzco was originally laid out in the form of a jaguar – a kind of living necropolis, *polis* as affirmation of death and life.)

Although frequent in the early Harappan art of the Indus Valley, the tiger is rarely visible as an icon in India until its masculinisation in Mughal times – quite strange, considering that Hinduism tended to find metaphysical uses for nearly every indigenous thing. In Hindu iconography it appears only occasionally as the vehicle for the Durga, the terrifying destroyer-goddess. There are, for example, no tigers in Vidyakara's *Treasury*, the great Sanskrit poetry anthology, where so much of Indian life and wildlife is represented. But among the jungle tribes the tiger was an active presence as devouring mother, fecund mother. "In

Akola," writes William Crooke in 1894, "the gardeners are unwilling to inform the sportsmen of the whereabouts of a tiger which may have taken up quarters in their plantation, for they have a superstition that a garden plot loses its fertility from the moment one of these animals is killed." And among the Gonds, wedding ceremonies were marked by the appearance of "two demoniacs possessed by Bagheswar, the tiger god" who "fell ravenously on a bleating kid, and gnawed it with their teeth till it expired."

There are no tigers in the Bible, and there were no tigers in medieval Europe – the bestiaries tended to classify them as birds or snakes. For nearly a thousand years, there were no tigers that look like tigers in Western art. So, when they began to be imported again into Europe from the animal market of Constantinople at the end of the 15th century, they were among the only creatures with no metaphysical meaning. In the absence of a fixed iconography, the West had to invent its allegorical tiger.

Shakespeare compares the murderous Queen Margaret (in *Henry VI Part 3*) to a tiger, and has Romeo express his rage in *yin* imagery:

The time and my intents are savage-wild,
More fierce and more inexorable far
Than empty tigers or the roaring sea.

But he also uses the tiger in its now-familiar masculine role: symbol of military valour. (Almost all the armies of the world are decked with tiger images.) Henry the Fifth, in his "Once more unto the breach, dear friends" speech:

But when the blast of war blows in our ears,
Then imitate the action of the tiger:
Stiffen the sinews, summon up the blood,
Disguise fair nature with hard-favored rage;
Then lend the eye a terrible aspect…
Now set the teeth and stretch the nostril wide,
Hold hard the breath and bend up every spirit
To his full height! On, on you noble English…

The Western image of the tiger was permanently altered in the 18th century by the reign of the Mughal prince Tipu Sultan (1750–1799), who was, in his mind, a tiger. He called himself the Tiger of Mysore. His throne was mounted on a full-size gilded tiger with rock-crystal eyes and teeth; its finials were tiger-heads set with rubies and diamonds; its canopy was tiger-striped with hammered gold. His soldiers dressed in tiger-patterned ("bubberee") jackets and kept their prisoners in tiger cages until it was time for them to be thrown to the tigers. Their cannons had tiger breech-blocks, their mortars were in the shape of crouching tigers, their rifles had tiger-headed stocks and hammers, their swords were engraved with tigers or forged in a striped blend of metals. Live tigers were chained to the palace doors. Tipu's handkerchiefs were striped; his banner read "The Tiger is God."

A stern moralist, Tipu instituted his version of Quranic law. He changed the calendar and all weights and measures, renamed all the cities and the towns, reformed every detail of daily existence from the way the markets were organised to the way crops were planted and gathered. He kept a book of his dreams. At night he slept on the floor on a coarse piece of canvas, and each morning he ate the brains of male sparrows for breakfast. He sponsored the arts.

He commanded an army of 140,000, sworn to wipe out the British. Prisoners were subjected to grotesque tortures: boiling oil, special devices for removing noses and upper lips. In his most brilliantly insidious punishment, he turned the enemy into its enemy: British soldiers were forced to cut off their foreskins and eat them.

He was the perfect Western nightmare of an Eastern despot, and the newspapers were full of Tipu. When an elderly servant was murdered in a siege, she was transformed into four hundred beautiful British virgins throwing themselves on swords rather than face the ravishment of Tipu's troops. In London, Tipu plays were a permanent attraction for thirty years. (The first, *Tippoo Sahib, or British Valour in*

India began running at Covent Garden on June 1, 1791. It was followed the next year by *Tippoo Sultan, or the Siege of Bangalore.*) When Tipu was finally slain and his capital Seringpatam captured by the British in 1798, it was cause for national celebration. Robert Ker Porter's 120-foot-long painting, "The Storming of Seringpatam," was mounted on the stage of the Lyceum and crowds paid a shilling each to view the great scene. Wilkie Collins in 1868 added an aura to his Moonstone by having it come from the plunder of Seringpatam, and as late as 1898 Sir Henry Newbolt had a best-selling epic poem on Tipu's defeat.

The tiger, then, took on a fearful androgyny: a masculine military ferocity within a dark Eastern feminine otherness. The tiger was, in the words of Capt. Williamson's *Oriental Field Sports* (1807), "the mottled object of detestation": an obstacle to progress. Its literal and metaphorical vanquishing became a British obsession. For a century boys' stories were full of man-eating tigers. With a short leap, the word "man-eater" was soon applied to women.

Blake's "tyger," according to the exegetes, stands for wrath, revolution, untamed energy and beauty, the romantic revolt of imagination against reason. It is associated with fire and smoke: "burning bright," roaming "in the redounding smoke in forests of affliction," "blinded by the smoke" issuing from "the wild furies" of its own brain. Numerous critics have pointed out that "The Tyger" of *Songs of Experience* was written in 1793, during the French Revolution. But it was also a time when the papers and theaters were crazy with tales of Tipu.

Did Blake ever see a real tiger? The Tower of London menagerie had been opened to the public in the middle of the century (price of admission: three ha'pennies or one dead dog or cat) and it frequently featured tigers. A new specimen was acquired in 1791, the year the first Tipu play opened. And when Blake lived at Fountain Court, the Strand, he could have strolled over to Pidcock's Exhibition of Wild Beasts, where tigers were often on display.

Pidcock and Blake form two sides of a tiger triangle: the third is George Stubbs, the first English painter of tigers. His "The Tyger," as Kathleen Raine points out in *Blake and the Tradition*, was first exhibited at the Society of Artists of Great Britain in 1769, at the same time and in the same building where the 12-year-old William Blake was studying drawing at Pars' school. It was Pidcock who sold Stubbs the dead tiger which the artist used for his last work, which bore the matchless title *The Comparative Anatomy of Humans, Chickens & Tigers.*

Stubb's "tyger" was probably the first the boy Blake had seen, but, like all the tigers Stubbs painted, is not an icon of untamed energy. It is a recumbent, noble but cuddly, large cat. (In contrast, his lions are always portrayed committing acts of terror in a storm-tossed landscape – as in the famous "Horse Attacked by a Lion," a motif Stubbs copied from

Roman statuary, which was itself a copy from Scythian art.) And when Blake came to illustrate his "The Tyger" the animal was so oddly passive and sweet, almost smiling, that some friends complained.

There is no doubt that Blake associated tigers with wrath and revolution, but it is interesting that Blake drew his physical image from Stubb's painting and the half-dead animals in the local cages; surely he could have imagined it otherwise. (Consider the terror of his flea.) Or is Blake's (and Stubbs') tyger meant to demonstrate the possibilities latent beneath a passive exterior, as yogis traditionally sat immobile on tiger-skin mats? Is the tyger's blank smile its most fearful symmetry?

It is quite probable that Blake had heard of the death of Sir Hector Munro's son, the most famous tiger-kills-Englishman story of the century. This account appeared in *The Gentleman's Magazine* in July 1793, the year "The Tyger" was composed:

To describe the awful, horrid and lamentable accident I have been an eye witness of, is impossible. Yesterday morning Mr Downey, of the [East India] Company's troops, Lieut. Pyefinch, poor Mr Munro and myself went onshore on Saugor Island to shoot deer. We saw innumerable tracks of tigers and deer, but still we were induced to pursue our sport, and did the whole day. At about half past three we sat down on the edge of the jungle, to eat some cold meat sent us from the ship, and had just commenced our meal, when Mr Pyefinch and a black servant told us there was a fine deer within six yards of us. Mr Downey and myself immediately jumped up to take our guns; mine was the nearest, and I had just laid hold of it when I heard a roar, like thunder, and saw an immense tiger spring on the unfortunate Munro, who was sitting down. In a moment his head was in the beast's mouth, and he rushed into the jungle with him, with as much ease as I could lift a kitten, tearing through the thickest bushes and trees, everything yielding to his monstrous strength. The agonies of horror, regret, and, I must say fear (for there were two tigers, male and female) rushed on me at once. The only effort I could make was to fire at him, though the poor youth was still in his mouth. I relied partly on Providence, partly on my own aim, and fired a musket. I saw the tiger stagger and agitated, and cried out so immediately. Mr Downey then fired two shots and I one more. We retired from the jungle, and, a few minutes after, Mr Munro came up to us, all over blood, and fell. We took him on our backs to the boat, and got every medical assistance for him from the *Valentine East India Main*, which lay at anchor near the Island, but in vain. He lived twenty four hours in the extreme torture; his head and skull were torn and broke to pieces, and he was wounded by the claws all over the neck and shoulders; but it was better to take him away, though irrecoverable than leave him to be devoured limb by limb. We have just read the funeral service over the body, and committed it to the deep. He was an amiable and promising youth. I must observe, there was a large fire blazing close to us, composed of ten or a dozen whole trees; I made it myself, on purpose to keep the tigers off, as I had always heard it would. There were eight or ten of the natives about us; many shots had been fired at the place, and much noise and laughing at the time; but this ferocious animal disregarded all. The human mind cannot form an idea of the scene; it turned my very soul within me. The beast was about four and a half feet high, and nine long. His head appeared as large as an ox's, his eyes darting fire, and his roar, when he first seized his prey, will never be out of my recollection. We had scarcely pushed our boats from the shore when the tigress made her appearance, raging mad almost, and remained on the sand as long as the distance would allow me to see her.

This scene of the humanly unthinkable, tiger and fire, may have inspired Blake, but it did most certainly inspire Tipu Sultan. Sir Hector, the boy's father (and ancestor of Hector Hugh Munro, "Saki," whose stories are full of animals attacking people) was the arch-enemy of Tipu's father, Haidar Ali. At the news of the boy's death – which Tipu gleefully interpreted as a sign that his fellow tigers were joining the struggle against the British – he ordered the construction of a large mechanical toy, now in the Victoria & Albert Museum, to commemorate the event.

It is a life-size wooden tiger crouched on a prone Englishman. They face each other; the man's left hand touches the tiger's face. They might be mistaken for lovers, but the tiger's teeth are sunk in the man's neck. ("Tipu Sultan," after all, means "Tiger Conqueror of Passion.") Wound up, the toy simultaneously emits roars and hideous groans. Keats, who had seen it in the East India Company offices when he was considering becoming a ship's doctor, called it the "Man-Tiger-Organ" in "The Cap and Bells." Flaubert, visiting the Great Exhibition in London in 1851, found it more fascinating than anything in the Crystal Palace. Marianne Moore wrote a poem about it: "This ballad still awaits a tiger-hearted bard."

After the fall of Seringpatam, tiger-killing became the standard measure in India of a Britisher's valour. And after the Empire forced peaceful co-existence onto the normally warring princely states, the Maharajahs could only display their power and manhood in British terms. No visit to a palace by a distinguished foreigner was complete without a tiger hunt. That the guest would be neither endangered nor disappointed, the tigers were often drugged beforehand with opium-laced meat to ensure a safe and unerring shot.

George Yule of the Bengal Civil Service killed 400 then stopped counting. Colonel Rice killed 93 in four years. Montague Gerard killed 227. The Maharajah of Surguja killed 1,150. The Maharajah Scindia killed at least 700. The guests of the Maharajah Scindia killed at least 200. The Maharajah of Gauripiur killed 500 then stopped counting.

As early as 1827, one Capt. Mundy writes:

Thus in the space of about two hours, and within sight of the camp, we found and slew three tigers, a piece of good fortune rarely to be met with in these modern times, when the spread of cultivation, and the zeal of the English sportsmen have almost exterminated the breed of these animals.

Emily Dickinson:

A Dying Tiger – moaned for Drink –
I hunted all the Sand –
I caught the Dripping of a Rock
And bore it in my Hand –

His Mighty Balls – in death were thick –
But searching – I could see

A Vision on the Retina
Of Water – and of me –

’Twas not my blame – who sped too slow –
’Twas not his blame – who died
While I was reaching him –
But ’twas – the fact that he was dead –

The Bali tiger: *extinct since 1937.*
The Caspian tiger: *extinct since 1970.*
The Java tiger: *extinct since 1979.*
The South China tiger: 59 left (all in captivity), *extinction inevitable.*
The Sumatra tiger: 400–500 left, *extinction possible.*
The Siberian tiger: 450–500 left, *extinction possible.*
The Malayan tiger: 600–800 left, *preservation possible.*
The Indo-Chinese tiger: 1200–1500 left, *declining rapidly*
The Bengal tiger: 2500–3000 left, *preservation possible.*

Tigers eat men only when they are starving, or are too old or sick to catch more elusive prey. In parts of India, it is believed that man-eating tigers are not tigers at all, but men who have transformed themselves into tigers to commit, for their purposes, masked acts of murder. These counterfeit tigers, the man-eaters, are recognisable to the villagers, as they would have been to Freud: they have no tails.

Jorge Luis Borges, from his half-century of blindness, writes:

In my childhood I was a fervent worshiper of the tiger…I used to linger endlessly before their cages at the zoo; I judged vast encyclopedias and books of natural history by the splendour of their tigers. (I still remember those illustrations: I who cannot rightly recall the eyes or the smile of a woman.)

Abu al-Anbas' Donkey

Abu al-Hassan Ali ibn al-Husain ibn Ali ibn Abd Allah al-Mas'udi, the tenth century historian from Baghdad, City of Peace, tells this story of a man named Abu al-Anbas, who lived during the reign of Mutawakkil, who abolished free thought and philosophical disputes, re-established the orthodoxy, severely enforced traditional religious values, gave little to the poor, built two palaces worth a hundred million dirhams, and devoted himself to board games, banquets, and each of his four thousand concubines:

Abu al-Anbas had a favourite donkey who suddenly died. One night the donkey appeared to him in a dream, and Abu spoke to him:

"Oh my donkey, didn't I always give you the coolest and freshest water? Wasn't I always sifting the barley I gave you? Why did you suddenly die?"

The donkey replied: "My master, I'm sorry. One day you stopped at the apothecary and the most beautiful donkey-girl passed by. I saw her; my heart was stricken, and I loved her with such a violent passion that in the end I succumbed to despair."

"Did you write a poem about her?"

"I did indeed. It goes:

My heart was stricken by a donkey-girl
As I waited for my master
By the door of the apothecary.
She enslaved me with her coy demeanor
And her two soft cheeks
The colour of *shanqarani*.
I died for her, for if I had lived
My passion would have only grown worse."

"Your poem is moving," said Abu al-Anbas, "but what does *shanqarani* mean?"

"Oh, that's an old word. You only hear it these days in donkey poetry."

Sex Objects

For those who object to sexual objectification, Sappho may present problems.
– *Poetry Flash* (San Francisco), reviewing Guy Davenport's *7 Greeks*

Zebra finches like their males with red legs and females with black legs, and are repelled by males with green legs or females with blue legs. A female Australian brush turkey is attracted to the male who builds her the largest nest, and is quite demanding: the nests can run to two tons. An Archbold bowerbird is especially smitten by a male capable of procuring rare King of Saxony bird of paradise blue feathers to feather the bower. A female tern prefers the male who presents her with the most fish; an emphid fly takes the one who produces the prettiest hollow silk balloons.

Guppies like their guppies bright orange; pupfish like their pupfish blue; squid like a squid whose skin changes colour. A cichlid looks at the inside of the throat, a fiddler crab at the single giant claw, turned blue, waving from the beach. A grackle wants a male who can sing more than one song. A female sage grouse will always take the best dancer, even if he has already mated with thirty others that day. A roach fish counts the number of bumps on a male's body. Female peacocks, as everyone knows, go for flashy tails. Swallows and widow birds and malachite sunbirds like their male tails long; great snipes want the whitest. Red jungle fowls look at the eyes and the comb, and couldn't care less about feathers. A cockroach watches the male do push-ups.

An aphid looks out for wings; the asexual variety don't have any. A male black grouse will mate with anything that looks vaguely like a female black grouse, even a wooden model. An Indian moon moth can smell a female miles away. Male hairless chimpanzees go for the pinkest and most swollen rear end. Bonobos – pygmy chimps – just have sex all the time. A female tortoise loves any male that butts her on the head; a rabbit any male who pees on her and shows his fluffy tail.

Sappho comes down to us only in the bits of papyrus used to wrap mummies, but some of the lineaments of her desire have survived. She wants – paraphrasing the Davenport translation – a woman slender as a young tree, with thin hands, and wrists like the wild rose. Eyes that are bold, or with a smiling brightness, beautiful feet, and something that has been lost in the lacunae, skin presumably, whiter than milk, whiter by far than an egg.

She loves violet breasts, and violet softness, the way the long pleats of a dress move, hair tied with red yarn, and a crown of flowers and dill on curly hair. The voice must be more melodious than a harp, more harmonious than lyres; a pleasing voice, with honey in its words. And an odour – though exactly which is now unknown. She is attracted to a country girl too ignorant to arrange her dress, or women wrapped in rich shaggy wool, with purple handkerchiefs, red dresses, robes the colour of peaches, with Asian deerhide shoes, or Asian leather shoes with Lydian patterns across the toes. A girl picking a flower just opened, softer than a fine dress, tenderer than a rose, graceful, decorous, suave, more golden than gold, like an apple, like a mountain hyacinth.

Sappho's mating grounds are a grove of apple trees, where horses munch on wildflowers, or on the cushions of soft beds. Her courtship rituals include drinking nectar in golden cups, plaiting garlands of roses and violets in one another's hair, leather phalluses, and aromatic oils. She falls asleep against the breast of a friend, [lacuna] slick with slime. Her desire is like wind in the mountain forests. Jealousy makes her tongue stick to her dry mouth, and a thin fire spread beneath her skin.

Haddock knock, crabs rasp, mosquitoes coo, swiftlets click, racket-tailed hummingbirds make a racket with their tails, male spiders pluck a rhythm on the female's web. A female canary must hear the song of her mate for her ovaries to develop; the more he sings, the faster this goes. The male echidna drugs the female with a mild poison from a spur on his heel. Crocodiles and minks simply rape.

Fungi have tens of thousands of sexes; earthworms are

hermaphrodites; slime molds have thirteen genders, all of which mate with each other in different ways. A slipper limpet floats on the sea as a male, then turns into a female when it attaches itself to a rock. Bdelloid rotifers are all female; they refresh their gene pool by eating their dead sisters. In the mating season, all the males of the Australian marsupial mouse die from the strain.

Sappho's most vivid fragment, one that needs no other lines above or below it, reads, in Davenport's translation, in its entirety:

"You make me hot."

A Frog Marriage

Each year, in the village of Pullipudupet, in southern India, a very young girl is selected to marry a frog. The customs of a traditional Indian wedding are followed. Half the village becomes the bride's family, and half the groom's. Accompanied by a marching band, the groom is led on a white horse to be welcomed at the bride's home. The entire nuptial ceremony is performed: the couple circles the sacred fire seven times; the edge of the bride's sari is tied to the groom's sash; their heads are held together by the priest. After the wedding banquet, the frog is released in a pond. The bride returns to her life as a schoolgirl. When she grows up, she is free to take a second, human husband.

An Indian journalist visited Pullipudupet to witness the ceremony. He asked the villagers why, each year, they marry a very young girl to a frog. No one knew; it was just what they had always done.

What Makes the Poet a Tick?

Written in response to the question, "What makes the poet tick?"

A tick is very small, the size of a single letter in a book. Who would notice? Its survival is dependent on a chance encounter with a host brushing past the leaves or grass. It wanders a body anonymously, searching for its place, and when it settles, it maintains its obscurity by emitting an anaesthetic so its host won't feel the impending bite. It cuts the skin with the pincers of its chelicerae and inserts the scary, serrated prong of its hypostome. From its midgut it injects a complex saliva with vasodilators to keep the veins and capillaries open, a whole family of anticoagulants to keep the blood flowing, agents to subdue threatening immune responses, and a kind of moisture-resistant glue to remain attached. It injects saliva, draws blood, injects saliva, draws blood, and grows fat, the size of a single letter in a chapter title. In its saliva are tens of thousands of bacteria; among them, the spirals of borrelia burgdoferi that induce facial paralysis, arthritis in the joints and numbness in the extremities, heartbeat irregularities leading to dizziness and fainting, perpetual sleepiness, and an inability to concentrate or to remember. When it has eaten, the tick drops off. The nourishment allows it to produce the hundreds of eggs it lays in the ground.

Where the Kaluli Live

In the thick forest where the Kaluli live, at the base of Mt. Bosavi in Papua New Guinea, it's hard to see far and space is mapped by sound:

kege kege kege
an Orange-faced Grackle

gubogubo gubogubo
a Black Sicklebird

ee-yehhhh-u
the Ornate Fruitdove

susulubee susulubee
the Superb Fruitdove

so-gaaaa gya gya gya
a Rufous-bellied Kookaburra

wek-woo wek-woo wek-woo
the Giant Cuckoodove at the top of
the waterfall *gulugulugulu*
splashing in the small pools below
kubu kubu kubu kubu

bawbawbawbawbaw Hornbills are flapping

teebo-teebo teebo-teebo
a Crested Pitohui

Hehhh a sick person wheezes

sawlawlawbeh sawlawlawbeh
the Trilling Kingfisher

haw-gooooo the wind goes through the forest
and a dried leaf drops *dehgeh!* from a breadfruit tree

ehhhhh the drone of the cicadas
deh deh deh deh deh
the sucking of the bats eating fruit

gehlehleh gehlehleh
a Hooded Butcherbird

godó godó godó the axe hits the tree
goooooo the tree falls through the air and
gaw! it crashes on the ground

sehleh sehleh knives are being sharpened on a stone
teketeketeke the anthropologist's typewriter
and *behdehbehdehbehdeh* his Honda generator

ti ti titi ti ti water drips after a rainstorm
and pours out
gugu gugu gugu gugu gugu
from the bamboo tubes on the roof of the longhouse

The Kaluli language is called Bosavi – named for the mountain, the collapsed cone of a dead volcano – and some of the birds speak it. The Black-breasted Woodswallow calls *bas-bas bas-bas*, "brother in law," to the Uniform Swiftlet, meaning that it's time to share food. The Black-throated Warbler says *seeyo-gogo-bayo seeyo-gogo-bayo*, "I'm staying right here." The Chanting Scrubwren chants *kaloo-yabe kaloo-yabe*, "someone is coming." The Brown Oriole, who is always female, has a foul mouth and insults the men passing by: *koo-halaideh koo-halaideh,* "what a hard cock." The Large-tailed Nightjar says, *noo-day-oo noo-day-oo*, "grandmother bring firewood." The Friarbird calls *dowo newo,* "father! mother!" for once some children were killed by an enemy and the Friarbird took their voices.

A Kaluli lives in two worlds: the visible world of people and the world of their reflections, where people live as wild pigs or cassowaries on the slopes of Mt. Bosavi. When a person dies, the reflection also disappears, and turns into a bird in the visible world. Birds see each other as people, and their calls are people talking to one other. The passage of life is from infant to bird.

Human songs are bird songs, and the words of a song are called "bird sound words." They are "turned-over words," words that are comprehensible but unlike anything in the spoken language, words that have a meaning underneath, on the other side. All the metaphors are based on birds, trees, lands, and waters. The songs are in the first person; the singer is alone after the death of a family member, or is travelling away from home. They describe a journey, each place-name bringing up nostalgic associations, for a tree is a home, a garden is food, a bird is a person, and life is a map and a song a path through it.

A great singer has a voice like a Pink-spotted Fruitdove or an Orange-bellied Fruitdove. The singer is a bird at the top of a waterfall, and the structure of a song is a waterfall. Songs that are poorly done have too much ledge before the water drops, or too much splashing, or they linger too long in the pool before moving on. A successful song is like water rushing over the rocks, and is one where the water keeps flowing far beyond where one can see.

In the old days, twenty years ago, before the airstrips and the missionaries and the oil drillers and the gold panners and the government officials, when the longhouses were lined with enemy skulls on pikes, the most important event was a ceremony of singing, the *gisalo*.

Each village lived in a single longhouse, and the longhouses were hours apart. Once or twice a year, a village would invite another to come sing. As night fell, the visitors arrived in a double line, carrying torches, and climbed the stairs into the suddenly silent longhouse of their hosts. Stretching the entire length of the interior, the two rows, after long moments of expectation, hissed loudly *ssssss*, like a tyre deflating, and abruptly sat down, revealing four singers, each identically and splendidly arrayed as birds, face and body painted red, eyes outlined in a black and white painted mask, Bird of Paradise feathers sprouting from armbands, head in an aureole of black Cassowary feathers with a single weighted and bobbing white feather in the middle, and a cascade of yellow palm leaf streamers arching from the waist up to the shoulders and down to the floor.

Three of the singers sat, and the first began at one end of the longhouse, singing softly, staring at the floor oblivious to the crowd, bouncing slightly with knees bent in the manner of a Giant Cuckoodove, accompanied by the monotonous and trance-inducing rattle of a string of mussel shells stretching from his hand to the floor. Moving slowly down the length of the longhouse, his song became louder and more intense as he sang of places familiar to his hosts and the sad events associated with those streams and trees and birds and fields. The hosts wept at the songs, and when their weeping became too unbearable, someone would grab a torch and shove it into the singer's chest or shoulder. Deep in the isolation of his song, the singer continued, unresponsive as he was burned again and again, until his song ended and another singer began, building the crescendos that would lead to his own burning.

The songs lasted until dawn, and the success of the evening was remembered in its retellings by how much the hosts were made to weep and how much the singing guests were burned. The last such night was in 1984.

In the Bosavi language, the word for "tomorrow" is the same as the word for "yesterday." The word no longer applies to Kaluli society, but the same birds who were once Kaluli

ee-yehhhh-u

ee-yehhh-u

susulubee susulubee susulubee

are still in the trees.

Teeth

To write about teeth. Just try.
– Elias Canetti

I had a pet rabbit who developed a dental problem. Her upper and lower incisors did not meet to grind each other down, and they kept growing. If left unattended, as sometimes happens in the wild, the teeth will grow to such length that they curve back into the rabbit's skull and pierce the brain. The veterinarian told me to buy a pair of special podiatrist's scissors and regularly clip her teeth.

The first time I tried, I botched the job. The teeth shattered; there was blood. An hour later I had to take a plane to another country, to attend one of those cultural conventions, always held abroad, where foreign governments treat otherwise obscure intellectuals to exorbitant hospitality.

I was met at the airport by an official, ushered to the front of the immigration line, and taken in a limousine to an elegant hotel. That night, in a suite on the fortieth floor, looking over the radiant expanse of the enormous city, marooned in the vastness of a bed designed for a free-love ashram, I couldn't sleep. The memory of the rabbit's bloody mouth kept me staring.

The next morning another limousine took me, a French poet, and a Chinese painter for a visit to a provincial capital. I already knew the place, so while the others toured the cathedral, I went to find a junk store on the Street of Frogs where, years before, I had bought a small, rusty mechanical device whose function no one has ever been able to ascertain.

Walking the colonial streets, I came across a crowd of a few hundred people and some television crews milling about, apparently waiting for something. I had read in the local paper that students had been protesting some university action; I assumed that the crowd was expecting a demonstration to march by. Half of the block was deserted. The people on either side had formed their own barriers, in order, I thought, to keep the sight lines clear for the cameras. There were no police, no agitation, nothing more than the familiar sight of a large group in the semi-comatose state of idle expectation.

A tourist, I was following a map, and my map told me that the shortest distance to where I was going was across the no man's land of the empty half-block. I walked along the sidewalk unhurriedly. People on either side began waving frantically, perhaps, I thought, because I was stumbling into what was to be the television picture. Then there was the crack of a shot, and I saw the brick wall a few inches from my head chip. Unalarmed, barely registering the event, not reacting with the "fight or flight" supposedly programmed in the genes, I quickened my pace, but did not run, toward the crowd on the other side. The next day I read that a student group was occupying the building; a rival group was trying to take it from them; the first group had placed snipers on the roof; two people had been shot that day.

The rabbit was all right. Her teeth resumed growing, and I periodically clipped with increasing expertise. I suddenly developed asthma, and tests showed that I was violently allergic to rabbits; but the rabbit stayed on: what else could I do, eat it? One night the following summer, at a house in the country, a Siberian husky belonging to a neighbour smashed through the small cage where the rabbit was living, mauled her to death, and then couldn't get out.

I thought of my pet rabbit a few years later, after reading a review of a book of mine in an academic journal. It ended: "Weinberger simply needs a freshman English class." The critic had been, considering his other remarks, uncharacteristically perceptive on this point. I had never had a freshman English class, having spent those years on the adolescent version of contemplating the void. So, in the American spirits of self-improvement and self-reliance, I decided to give myself some lessons, and assigned myself an essay on a favourite pet; it seemed the thing to do.

I sent it to an old friend, a writer of short fictions who occasionally teaches the writing of short fiction. She thought the composition vague and pointless; if I was trying to draw a parallel between myself and the rabbit as victims, it wasn't very clear. This connection had never occurred to me; I thought I was writing an associative narrative somewhat in the style of Felisberto Hernández, albeit with less charm. Discouraged, I abandoned the essay.

Recently, I came across this challenge from Elias Canetti, the most obstinate of writers, who was, insufferably, always right. There have been notable writers who were doctors, but no writers I can remember who were dentists, although both practise oral arts. The decay of the tooth has never been as moving as the decay of the body. More exactly, the sickness of the tooth and its subsequent extraction have tended to be viewed allegorically rather than as revelatory of human nature. Toothlessness is a political metaphor for powerlessness, and was once a Christian metaphor for the absence of licentiousness; the two combined to become the Freudian dream symbol of castration. Toothache, said Petrarch, is a reminder of death, which is eternal life.

The teeth of my pet rabbit were neither allegorical nor particularly revelatory. She was toothsome, but not powerful; she may well have been licentious, as reputation has it, but she lacked the companionship of her kind. I hope her teeth did not ache, but who can know the aches of a rabbit? As it is said, almost, the heart of a rabbit is a dark forest.

The Laughing Fish

In *The Ocean Made of Streams of Story*, the 11th-century Kashmiri precursor to *The Thousand and One Nights* as a vast compendium of nested tales, there is an image that reappears in insomnia. The King sees one of his wives leaning over a balcony and talking to a Brahmin. In a fit of jealousy, he orders the Brahmin to be put to death. As the man is being led through the town to his execution, a fish, lying in a stall in the market, bursts out laughing. The King stops the execution to find out why the fish laughed. (The reason is that the Brahmin is completely innocent, while the harem of the King's dissolute wives is full of men disguised as women…but that's another story.)

In a footnote, the annotator of the 1923 edition of the C.H. Tawney translation, the seemingly omniscient N.M. Penzer, M.A., F.R.G.S., F.G.S, cites an article in the 1916 volume of the *Journal of the American Oriental Society* on "Psychic *Motifs* in Hindu Fiction, and the Laugh and Cry *Motif*." Its author, identified only as "Professor Bloomfield," classifies the various kinds of laughter found in that literature: "There is the cry and laugh together, and each separately. Of laughter by itself, there is the laugh of joy, of irony, malice, trickery, and triumph. Then there is the sardonic laugh, the enigmatic, fateful laugh (sometimes with ironic humor in it), and finally there is the laugh of mystery, as in the case of the fish that laughed." The taxonomy seems more human than Hindu, but in any event, the category of mere mystery for the laughing fish is weak.

With the exception of the shark, fish have never been given any human attributes. No fish is as contented as a cow, sly as a fox, wise as an elephant or an owl, industrious as a bee, faithful as a turtledove, self-sacrificing as a pelican, or even as lowly as a worm. Aesop, though he came from a maritime culture, has only one talking fish in his hundreds of fables: an undersized pickerel who tries to persuade the fisherman to throw him back. Without any particular personality, it merely argues for its survival.

Adam doesn't know the names of fish. He is shown all the beasts of the field and the fowls of the air and – the theological questions are unresolvable – either names them (by what process and in what language?) or calls them by the names they already have (which assumes a divine language, now lost, where the signifier was not random). But no fish are hauled up before him in Eden. His ignorance continues on as a blank area in the human brain: the otherwise multilingual often struggle to translate the fish on a menu.

Lawrence, in a celebrated poem in *Birds, Beasts and Flowers*, writes: "Fish, oh Fish,/ So little matters!/...To be a fish!// So utterly without misgiving/…/ Loveless and so lively/…/…soundless, and out of contact./ They exchange no word, no spasm, not even anger./ Not one touch./ Many suspended together, forever apart,/ Each one alone with the waters…" The poem takes six pages to say: "They are beyond me, are fishes."

The beyond of the fishes may be why watching them is the most peaceful activity on earth, floating above them with a mask and snorkel. (A public aquarium is contaminated by the presence of the sounds of the other people; an aquarium at home always remains in the context of the other objects of one's life; scuba is inextricable from its respiratory anxiety.) More than merely watching bright-coloured creatures dart around, its tranquility comes from its total lack of human association. Fish have no connection to our emotional life: unlike the other creatures, they do not mate (as Lawrence, naturally, keeps repeating), they hardly squabble, they do not care for their young. Even insects work. A fish swims and eats, is pure movement and beauty. It inhabits a world we can only watch weightlessly, soundlessly, and behind glass. To watch fish is to not be oneself. Even in a magnificent landscape, we inhabit that landscape; it is full of smells and sounds and imagery that connect to countless thoughts, feelings, memories, artworks. Standing under a night sky inevitably leads to thoughts of one's significance in the universe. But a fish neither reflects nor questions our existence. A fish is and we are: to become engrossed in watching fish is to forget that we are, but without, as mystics experience, becoming part of what we observe. The world is everything that is not the case. A laughing fish would not only be like us, it would care enough to laugh at us, a terrifying thing.

Lizards

In Hudson, Wisconsin, Daniel O'Connell, proprietor of the O'Connell Family Funeral home, and his young assistant were found shot to death. It was suspected that the murders were the work of a local religious group with an unfortunate name, the Rest of Jesus Ministry, which had recently sent a memorandum to its members, titled "Prepare for War," in its continuing campaign against the practice of embalming, and had mailed letters to local undertakers, addressed to "My people who deal with the corpses."

The letter read, in part: "Respect for the body comes by wrapping it in white linen and laying it in a place prepared. Pickling of the body, by the draining of the blood, by the draining of its leftover blood is an abomination to Me and this practice Must Cease! Failure to comply to cease from the pickling of the body and the adoration of the dead will bring a judgment of much death upon this land."

Three weeks earlier, the police in Newark, Delaware, alerted by neighbours, broke into the apartment of one Ronald J. Huff. There they found seven Nile monitor lizards, each about six feet long, feeding on his corpse.

Lizards' feet look like human hands; in many places, people used to be lizards, until the day when their tails were cut off, their noses pushed in, and they began to walk upright. Small lizards are lively youths; the large ones venerable sages. They like to stare at people with their unblinking eyes, and listen to human conversation. They are messengers of the gods; they warn against dangers; like storks they bring babies; they are where the soul or the shadow-soul or the dream-soul resides.

The Kayapo, who live in the jungles of northeastern Brazil, say, or used to say, that once, before a huge feast, when the men were gone hunting, a lizard came to a young woman and made love to her night after night. Her mother could hear her talking, and suspected a man, but couldn't see his face, so she got up before dawn, and hid behind a door. She watched a pino lizard scurry out and climb a tree.

The mother told her husband and they built a fire at the base of the tree. Many lizards died, but so many leapt over the fire and into a nearby brook that the brook became the size of a river. The parents followed the river until they came to a village of large houses. It was the village of the lizards, and the lizards had turned into Christians, Christian people, and they were the first Christians seen in the Kayapo forest.

The girl eventually had a son, who turned into a lizard at night, and whom her grandparents wanted to kill, so mother and son escaped and became Christians, and went to live in the Christian lizard village.

A monitor lizard can smell carrion seven miles away. A female lays her eggs in a termite nest and then returns to the exact spot exactly nine months later to break open the nest to let the hatchlings escape. A monitor lizard can count to six. In the Andaman Islands, the monitor lizard is, or was, a female god that is the northeast wind that brings the cyclones. The cyclones come when the lizard wind is angry, and three things make her angry: melting or burning beeswax; cutting or digging up yams and other roots at certain times of the year; killing a cicada, or making a noise when the cicadas are singing in the morning or evening.

The Kayapo do not embalm or preserve the dead. They bury them in a pit, sitting, facing east, and pile their possessions on top of the mound. These the dead take with them to the village of the dead, where everyone sleeps all day and moves around at night, where the old become young and those who died young are old, and where the only food is dirt and lizards.

Han Yu's Address to the Crocodiles

On the 24th day of the 4th month of the year 819, Han Yu, Governor of Chao-zhou (Canton), instructed his officer Qin Ji to take one sheep and one pig and hurl them into the deep waters of the river Wu as an offering of food for the crocodiles. When the crocodiles had gathered, Han Yu addressed them in the following manner:

In ancient times, it was the practice of our former Emperors to set the mountains and swamps ablaze, and with nets, ropes, spears and knives drive beyond the four seas all reptiles, snakes and malevolent creatures noxious to man. Later, Emperors arose who were of lesser power, unable to maintain an Empire of such vastness. Even the Centre was forsaken, let alone here in Chao, between the five peaks and the sea, 10,000 miles from the capital. In that chaos, you crocodiles crept back and multiplied. It was a natural situation under those circumstances.

Now, however, a true Son of Heaven has ascended the throne: one godlike in wisdom, benevolent in peace, merciless in war. All within the four seas and the six directions is his to rule, administered by governors and prefects whose territories pay tribute to furnish the great sacrifices to Heaven and Earth, at the altars of our ancestors and all the gods.

These governors and crocodiles cannot share common ground.

The governor, under the command of the Son of Heaven, has been entrusted with the protection of this land and of its people. But you, bubble-eyed crocodiles, you are not satisfied with the river depths. You take every opportunity to seize and devour people and their livestock, bears and boars, stags and deer, to extend your bellies and multiply your line. You are thus in discord with the governor, and seemingly rival his authority.

A governor, no matter how feeble, could never bow his head, humble his heart before a crocodile, nor could he stand by in trepidation, shamed before his officers and subjects, acting in an unworthy manner during the existence granted him in this place. Therefore, having received the command of the Son of Heaven to come here as his deputy, he must contend with you, crocodiles. If you have understanding, hear then the governor's words:

To the south of this province lies the great sea. In it there are places for creatures as great as the whale or shark, insignificant as the shrimp or crab. All there have a home in which to live and eat. If you left this morning, crocodiles, you would be there tonight. Thus I will make this agreement with you:

Within three days, you must take your hideous brood and head south to the sea, thereby submitting to this appointed deputy of the Son of Heaven. If three days are insufficient, I will allow five. If five days are insufficient, I will allow seven. If, however, after seven days you still linger, with no indication of departure, I will assume that either you have heard and have refused to obey the words of your governor, or else that you are vacant and without reason, incapable of understanding even when a governor speaks to you.

Those who defy the deputies of the Son of Heaven, who do not listen to their words or refuse to accept them, who from stupidity or lack of intellect harm people and the lesser creatures – such as these will be put to death. The governor will select skilled officers and men who, with strong bows and poison-tipped arrows, shall summarily end this matter, not ceasing, crocodiles, till you all are slain. I therefore recommend that you do not forestall your decision until it is too late.

That night, a violent storm struck the province. When it subsided, some days later, it was discovered that the crocodiles were gone. They were not seen again for a hundred years, when the Empire was again in ruin.

Note

Han Yu (768–824): poet, prose master, the leading Tang Confucianist and vehement anti-Buddhist. His "Address" falls at the midpoint of the downward spiral of communication between man and other species from the tribal to the metropolitan.

The Confucian world is a wheel: the Emperor is the hub, his power and authority radiating outward through bureaucratic spokes to encompass everything within the empire. In times of chaos, when the Emperor is weak, when "the center does not hold," everything is possible and in flux. In times of order, each has a fixed place. Thus the crocodiles here are literally trespassers, to be treated like criminals, outlaws from the cosmic contract.

Between the sacred tribal fellowship of hunter and hunted and the metropolitan view of animals as meat-objects or fur-objects or art-objects or obstacles, lies this curious Confucian bureaucratic response. Han Yu reads the (not quite apprehended) criminals their rights. They may voluntarily accept the order of the world; if they do not, then divine justice, the word of the Emperor will be executed. It may well be the last time that men offered the natural world respectfully negotiated terms of surrender.

A Man-Tiger

The *Huai Nan Tzu*, an encyclopedic book from the 2nd century B.C.E., tells the story of a man from ancient times, Kung Yu-ai, who for seven days was turned into a tiger. Fur grew over his body; his hands turned into claws; his teeth were those of a wild animal. His brother went to take a look; the tiger leapt and mauled him to death.

The tiger never knew he had once been a man. The man never knew he would someday be a tiger. The tiger was happy being a tiger, following his tiger nature. The man was happy being a man, following his human nature. Both enjoyed the happiness of being themselves, and neither suspected that they were equally happy as something entirely different.

The Rhinoceros

From the newspaper *Ka Lama Hawai'i*, Lahaina Luna, February 21, 1834:

NO KA LAEHAOKELA

[ABOUT THE RHINOCEROS]

1. O ka Elepani wale no ka mea i oi aku kona nui mamua o ka Laehaokela. Eono paha kapuai kona kiekie a he umikumamalua ka loihi, a he umikumamaha kekahi.

[The Elephant is the only animal larger than the Rhinoceros. The Rhinoceros is about six feet in height and twelve feet in length. Some reach fourteen feet.]

2. Ua loihi loa kona kino, a ua nui; ua pokole kona mau wawae; ua manoanoa hoi; a ua kaumaha; ua palahalaha kona pepeiao, a ku pono iluna; ua oi aku kona lehelehe luna mamua o ka lehelehe lalo; ua uuku kona mau maka ua mimino nui loa kona ili, e like me ka lole manoanoa,

i hoalualuia; ua loihi kona nuku, a malaila kona pepeiaohao nui, ikaika loa; a ua pokole kona kapuai, a ekolu no manamana.

[His body is very long and large; his legs are short; he is thick and heavy; his ears are flat yet stand straight up; his upper lip protrudes over his lower lip; his eyes are small and his skin is very wrinkled, like thick cloth that is gathered; his snout is long, and on it is his large, extremely sturdy horn; he has short, three-toed feet.]

3. O kona pepeiaohao hookahi, ma ka nuku, oia kona haokela; oia hoi kona mea kaua aku i ka Liona, a me ka Elepani, a me ka Tiga, a me na ilio e ae. No kona ikaika loa, e hiki no ia ia ke hou aku i ka laau nui a puka no i kela aoao, e like me ka hou ana o ke kui laau iloko o ka uwala.

[As for that single hard protuberance upon his snout, that is his great horn; it is the weapon with which he battles the Lion, the Elephant, the Tiger, and other four-legged animals. Because of his great strength, he is able to pierce a large piece of wood clean through, like a nail poking through a sweet potato.]

4. O ka mauu ka ai a ka Laehaokela, a e ai no hoi ia i ke kakalaioa a me ka lala laau, a me ke ko, a me ke kurina, a me na mea maka a pau e like me ka nahelehele.

[The Rhinoceros eats grass, but will also eat thorny brambles, tree branches, sugar cane, corn, and all other green things such as bushes.]

5. Ua oi kona lehelehe luna, a e hiki no ia ia ke o aku ia mea, i hookahi kapuai paha, a me ia no ia i holiili ai kana ai.

[His upper lip is pointed, and he is able to stick it out reaching perhaps a foot or so, and that is how he gathers his food.]

6. Aole ia e kolohe mai ke kolohe ole iaku ia, aka, ina kii aku kekahi ilio ia ia, a o ke kanaka paha, alaila, hihiu loa la Laehaokela, aole hoi he mea i oi aku ka ikaika i ka hakaka ana. No kona ikaika, a no kona akamai i ka hou aku me kona haokela, aole hiki ka Elepani ke lanakila maluna ona, a he hapa ka makau o ke Tiga i ka Elepani, he nui kona makau i ka Laehaokela.

[He will not bother you if he is left alone, but should another animal, or human perhaps, approach him, the Rhinoceros becomes extremely vicious, and there is nothing stronger in a fight. Because he is so strong and skilled in wielding his great horn, the Elephant cannot triumph over him. The fear a Tiger feels for the Elephant is but half of what he feels for the Rhinoceros.]

7. No ka manoanoa loa o kona ili, aole e komo nui ka maiuu o ka Liona a me ke Tiga.

[Because his skin is so thick, the claws of the Lion or Tiger will barely pierce him.]

8. Aia maloko o na ululaau o Asia a me Aferika kahi e holo nui ai ka Laehaokela; ma kahi haahaa ma kahi wai; no ka mea, makemake loa ia e haluku maloko o na kiolepo, e like me ka puaa.

[The Rhinoceros roams mainly in the forests of Asia and Africa, in low-lying wet areas, because he loves to wallow in mud holes, as does the pig.]

9. E hiki no ke hoolaka iki i ka Laehaokela, a noho malie ia maloko o ka pa; e hiki no ke ao iki aku ia ia i ka hana. Aole nae ia i akamai, ua hemahema no, kokoke like me ka puaa.

[One is able to tame a Rhinoceros a little so that he will live quietly in an enclosure; it is also possible to teach him to perform some tasks. However, he is not intelligent but rather inept, almost like the pig.]

10. E ai no na Inikini a me ko Aferika i kona io, a olelo lakou, ua ono.

[Indians and Africans eat of his flesh and claim it to be delicious.]

11. He mea maikai loa kona ili, no ka manoanoa a no ka oolea. O kona haokela, he laaulapaau ia, i ka poe naaupo.

[His hide is very good both for its thickness and durability. His great horn is of medicinal value, according to the ignorant.]

12. Makemake no ia, e hele wale me ka mehameha; no kona hupo loa, aole lealea ke hele pu me kekahi Laehaokela. O ka haluku maloko o ko lepo, o ka ai i ka ai, a me ka hiamoe, o kana mau mea lealea no ia.

[He likes to travel alone, and because of his extreme stupidity, he does not find pleasure in travelling with another Rhinoceros. Wallowing in mud, eating, and sleeping are his pleasures.]

13. E kanalua paha kekahi me ka ninau mai, "Ua hanaia ke Laehaokela, i mea aha?"

[Uncertain, one might ask, "Why, then, was the Rhinoceros created?"]

II

The first rhinoceros in Europe in the 1300 years after the fall of the Roman empire arrived in Lisbon on May 20, 1515, a gift from Sultan Muzaffar II of Gujarat to Afonso de Albuquerque, governor of Portuguese India, as a consolation prize, after refusing to allow the Portuguese to build a fortress on the island of Diu. Albuquerque, in turn sent it on to his king, Dom Manuel I, "The Fortunate," a connoisseur of the exotic. Dom Manuel quickly put to the test Pliny's famous assertion that the rhinoceros and the elephant are deadly enemies, and that the rhinoceros would run under the legs of the elephant, ripping open the tender underbelly with its horn. Both were placed in a rink on the third of June. The rhinoceros stood motionless, and the elephant walked away.

Nevertheless, the rhinoceros was a sensation. Within two months, a doctor in Florence published a paean to it, in twenty-one stanzas of ottava rima. The Emperor Maximilian had a rhinoceros drawn in the margin of his prayer book; Raphael placed one in a fresco of the Creation of the Animals in the Vatican. Someone, it is not known who, sent a sketch of the animal to Albrecht Dürer in Nuremberg, whose heavily armored version – Dürer was a designer of armor – remained the standard image of the rhinoceros for centuries, though Dürer never saw one.

In December 1515, Dom Manuel demonstrated his piety by

sending the rhinoceros as a gift to Pope Leo X. The rhinoceros was dressed as a bride with a gilt chain and a green velvet harness decorated with roses and carnations and edged with fringe. On the way, the ship stopped at an island off Marseilles, where the rhinoceros was presented to the King and Queen of France as part of an elaborate battle pageant, with oranges for cannonballs. The ship sank in a storm on the Genoa coast in January. The carcass of the animal was found on the beach, stuffed, and taken to Rome.

The second rhinoceros in Europe came to Lisbon in 1579, as a gift to the Spanish King Philip II, who now ruled Portugal and had temporarily moved his court from Madrid. An Italian in the court wrote a letter home that the rhinoceros is "beyond the imagination of anyone who has not seen it"; he compared it to Petrarch's Laura.

When Philip returned to Madrid in 1583, the rhinoceros went with him, and was often displayed in the garden of the Escorial. It was described by a visitor as "curious, melancholy, and sad," and after it suddenly charged and overturned a carriage carrying royal guests, its horn was cut off and its eyes put out.

In 1607, the Reverend Edward Topsell, who had never seen a rhinoceros, wrote that it is "a beast in every way admirable; both for the outward shape, quantity, and greatness, and also for inward courage, disposition, and mildness." Topsell, somewhat contradictorily, repeated the legend, taken from the unicorn, that the wild beast could only be captured by a virgin maiden, for the smell of virginity makes it fall asleep. Marco Polo, who had seen rhinoceroses in captivity in China, had said this wasn't true.

By the time of the third rhinoceros in Europe, 1684, the Spanish and Portuguese empires had waned and the British was rising, so the animal was sent to London. Typical of the new world order, it was not a bauble for kings or popes, but a commercial enterprise, on exhibit for twelve pence a head, or two shillings if you wanted to attempt to ride it. The rhinoceros died within two years.

The fourth rhinoceros in Europe, in 1739, was also in London and also a commercial spectacle, the price having now risen, after fifty years, to two shillings sixpence for a look. James Parsons gave a detailed report to the Royal Society: "He appeared very peaceable in his Temper; for he bore to be handled in any Part of his Body; but is outrageous when struck or hungry, and is pacified in either Case only by giving him Victuals." Parsons notes its extraordinary sensitivity to "any Noise or Rumour in the Street"; in 18th-century London, these must have been considerable. "In his Outrage he jumps about, and springs to an incredible height, driving his Head against the Walls of the Place with great Fury and Quickness, notwithstanding his lumpish Aspect."

The fifth rhinoceros in Europe, perhaps the most famous rhinoceros who ever lived, the cause of a continental "rhinomania," was trapped in the Kingdom of Assam, presented to the director of the Dutch East India Company in Bengal, and sent to Holland in 1741. It toured Europe for sixteen years.

In Berlin, Frederick the Great viewed the rhinoceros at a fish stall in the Spittelmarkt and left a tip of eighteen ducats. He later insisted that his friend Voltaire strike out a sentence in the *Philosophical Dictionary*, arguing against the Newtonian theory of the "intelligent design" of all creatures: "Modern natural philosophers have found God in the folds of the skin of the rhinoceros." Voltaire complied.

In Vienna, the Empress Maria Theresa came down from her country house, Schloss Schönbrunn, to see it, and made its owner, a Dutch sea captain, a Baron of the Empire. The boy Archduke Karl Joseph was painted on a miniature holding a book with a drawing of a rhinoceros. In Dresden, at the Red Stag near the Prina Gate, Augustus III, King of Poland and Elector of Saxony, and his heir, the sickly Elector Prince, came for a viewing. In Leipzig, the popular hack poet, Christian Fürchtegott Gellert wrote a poem about it, and the scholar Friedrich Gotthilf Freytag, a pamphlet in Latin with quotations in Greek. In Mannheim, the Elector Palatine, Carl Theodor, came with his heir presumptive, Duke Christian IV of Zweibrücken, the Duke's brother, Prince Frederick Michael, and their wives. In Strasbourg, three commemorative medals were struck; in Nuremberg, a medal was struck weighing 5,000 pounds. In Würzburg it was given the nickname "Miss Clara," which stuck. In Versailles, its owner tried to sell it for 100,000 écus to Louis XV, but the king refused.

Ormolu rhinoceros clocks, coins, ribbons à la rhinocéros, rhinoceros dummies at royal wedding pageants, rhinoceros hairdos with a feather horn. Casanova tells an improbable story of his current mistress mistaking the rhino's dark-skinned and "very masculine" attendant for the rhinoceros itself; Jean-Baptiste Oudry paints it for the collection of the Duke of Mecklenburg-Schwerin; Buffon includes it in his *Natural History*.

In Lyons, rumours that it had killed five people and then died from the "heat of love"; in Naples the Marquis d'Argenson spreads the rumour that it had perished in a shipwreck off the coast. Rome, Florence, Bologna, Venice for the Carnival. Pietro Longhi and his school are commissioned to paint it many times: surrounded by visitors in masks, standing next to the Irish giant, Magrath. In London, Miss Clara is exhibited as an "Uncommon Natural Curiosity", along with two dwarfs, a Negro contortionist, and a crocodile. Warsaw, Danzig, Cracow, Copenhagen.

Rhinos on Gobelin tapestries, in a fresco in the Garden Room of the Schloss Ober St. Veit, rhinos on delftware drug jars with the arms of the Worshipful Society of Apothecaries, on Sinceny faience table tops, on the Northumberland Service of Meissen porcelain, Chelsea oval dishes, tureen stands for the Japanese Service of Frederick the Great, Saxon enameled humpens, Schapen glass bun-footed beakers, and Dresden goblets with half-nude Moorish girls; bronze and marble sculptures of rhinos, and shell collages; rhinos on inlaid Marquetry card tables, Venetian green lacquer bureau-cabinets, boulle table tops, chessboards of tortoiseshell and mother-of-pearl, gold and piqué snuffboxes, *verre églomisé* panels on giltwood stands, rhino bookplates and title-pages, rhino allegorical paintings. The colours of the Saxony-Altenburg Infantry Regiment are a rhinoceros standing by a palm tree, with the legend "Non recedo nisi vincam," "I return not unless I have conquered."

The sixth rhinoceros in Europe arrived in France in 1790, after an arduous journey in which it was regularly massaged with fish oil to keep its skin moist. It lived a quiet life alone in Versailles for twenty-three years, with its own shelter and pool of water, rarely noticed, and unaffected by the Revolution and the Terror.

The seventh rhinoceros in Europe was acquired in 1790 for Pidcock's Exhibition of Wild Beasts at Exeter Change in the Strand in London, the place where William Blake may have seen his only tiger. It was displayed with "three stupendous ostriches," and George III summoned it for a viewing at the Queen's Lodge. It died within two years. The Reverend W. Bingley wrote: "His docility was about equal to that of a tolerably tractable pig. He was very fond of sweet wines, of which he would often drink three or four bottles in the course of a few hours. His voice was not much unlike the bleating of a calf. It was most commonly exerted when the animal observed any person with fruit or other favorite food in his hand. During the severe illness which preceded his death, this noise, but in a more melancholy tone, was almost constantly heard, occasioned doubtless by the agonies he underwent." The animal was stuffed and continued to be exhibited around England for many years.

The eighth rhinoceros in Europe, acquired by Pidcock in 1799, was soon sold to the Emperor of Germany, Francis II. Awaiting shipment across a war-torn Europe, rarely seen, it died a few months later, in a stable on Drury Lane.

III

Editorial note, *Journal of the Royal African Society,* April, 1924:

The British people have in the last hundred years wrought great changes for the better in Africa. They have abolished slavery for the negro and have induced other great nations of white people to do the same. They have taken the leading part in placing the interior of Africa on the map; have produced that remarkable work *The Flora of Tropical Africa*, and added enormously to our knowledge of African peoples and their history, African languages, and African zoology. But in one direction they will have incurred the severe blame of civilised posterity: their reckless, sometimes brutal extermination of the more interesting African mammals. Their latest victim is the white or square-lipped rhinoceros. This truly remarkable and harmless monster a hundred years ago swarmed in Southern Africa between the Orange River and Zululand, the course of the Zambezi, and Southern Angola. Livingstone met with it on the Upper Zambezi close to the Congo watershed. Speke and Grant obtained specimens of its horns in the west of Uganda. But in Trans-Zambezian Africa, Boer and mainly British sportsmen steadily shot it down (though it was of little or no use for any purpose), until at the beginning of the twentieth century its numbers were reduced in all South Africa to a herd of twenty which found refuge in North Zululand.

In Equatorial East Africa the white rhinoceros was thought to be extinct; but about 1907 or 1908 it was re-discovered, north of Uganda in the southern part of the Bahr-el-ghazal Province. Here, close to the Nile, near Lado, Colonel Roosevelt was permitted to shoot two or three specimens for American museums.

In 1919 a British official on the Anglo-Egyptian Sudan computed its numbers at not quite 3,000. Up to that period it was placed under strict protection by the Sudan authorities. Two or three years later this protection was removed or not enforced, and Dr. Cuthbert Christy now estimates the extent of its "killing out" so highly that he declares there are scarcely one hundred of these beasts left alive. A Government Game Ward in South Africa accuses the Natal Government of similar negligence or indifference, and declares that the white rhinoceroses in the Zululand preserve have been reduced by British game-killers from twenty to a doubtful twelve. One man alone killed four. What angers the American naturalists especially is the silence of the British press while the white rhinoceros is being done to death.

Mongalla, 1st August, 1924
To the Editor of the Journal of the Royal African Society.

Dear Sir,
[…]
This is a most unfair attack on the Game Preservation Department of the Sudan and on the officials stationed there. The exceptional co-operation of all officials with the Game Preservation Department make the carrying out of game laws in the Sudan the admiration of sportsmen and naturalists and the disgust of all butchers of game. No

American or Press aid is necessary for the protection of the White Rhino. In fact he was probably never so numerous as he is to-day since the Lado was administered by the Sudan Government.

Dr. Christy's alleged "killing out," therefore, requires some amplification in order to be taken seriously by anyone possessing even an elementary knowledge of the subject and I challenge him to support his statement by facts.

I remain, Sir,

Your obedient servant,

G. G. CARPENTER,

Captain,

The Suffolk Regiment,

attached, Equatorial Battalion,

East Africa

February 6th, 1925

To the Editor of the Journal of the Royal African Society.

Dear Sir,

My attention has just been drawn to a letter, dated August 1924, from Capt. Carpenter, stationed at Mongalla in the Upper Sudan, with reference to the subject of the regrettable "killing out" of the

White Rhinoceros, and published in the *Journal* of October last.

Owing to my being in America from June to November the letter in question escaped my notice, and I hasten to repudiate any desire to attack or criticise the Sudan Game Preservation Department, with which Capt. Carpenter apparently wishes to embroil me. He does not mention where "Dr. Christy's sweeping statement" is to be found in print, if published at all, nor has he a good word to say for the White Rhinoceros, which most of us who are aware of the facts know is a diminishing species, though still a fairly common animal over a wide range of country between the Upper Nile and French Equatorial Africa. Few persons have travelled up and down over more of this particular region than I have, and I am able to tell Capt. Carpenter how the case for the White Rhinoceros stands.

Everywhere he is decreasing in numbers, the natives south-west of the Nile-Congo Divide spearing a great many annually for the price of their horns. Throughout the Welle region of the Congo, after the annual grass fires have opened up the country, the bleached bones of these animals are common and conspicuous objects amongst the burnt and blackened surroundings. [...]

If Capt. Carpenter wishes to know what I myself have said on the subject he may refer to the chapter on the White Rhinoceros in my *Big Game and Pygmies*, published in April 1924. [...]

No large animal in my opinion is less harmful, less dangerous, and more easily shot than is this comparatively defenceless walking gargoyle of the bush.

I am, Sir,
Yours faithfully,
CUTHBERT CHRISTY

IV

African black rhino, c. 1900: 2,000,000 – 3,000,000.
African black rhino, c. 1970: 65,000.
African black rhino, c. 2000: 3,600.

Between 1970 and 1987, 85% of the world's population of rhinos were killed.

Northern white rhino: 25 left, *extinction inevitable.*
Javan rhino: 60 left, *extinction inevitable.*
Sumatran rhino: 300 left, *extinction probable.*
Indian rhino: 1700 left, *declining rapidly.*
Southern white rhino: 4,600 left, *preservation possible.*

V

In the British Library there is a box of fragments and dust from a birch bark scroll buried two thousand years ago on the Jalalabad Plain, west of the Khyber Pass. It is the oldest known Buddhist text, written in the Gandharan language. Some of the chips contain only a single letter, but the scholars have pieced them together to reconstruct a sutra:

Doing no violence to living things, not even a single one of them, wander alone like a rhinoceros.

Affection comes from the company of people, misery comes from affection, wander alone like a rhinoceros.

The old bamboo is entangled, the young shoot is unattached, wander alone like a rhinoceros.

A deer goes to eat where it wants to eat, wander alone like a rhinoceros.

Give up your children and your wives and your money, wander alone like a rhinoceros.

Everyone wants your attention, wander alone like a rhinoceros.

Two bright bangles on an arm clang, a single bangle is silent, wander alone like a rhinoceros.

A bird who has torn the net, wander alone like a rhinoceros.

Fire does not return to what it has burnt, wander alone like a rhinoceros.

A tiger is not alarmed by sounds in the forest, wander alone like a rhinoceros.

Cold and heat, hunger and thirst, wander alone like a rhinoceros.

With eyes cast down, wander alone like a rhinoceros.

At home anywhere, wander alone like a rhinoceros.

Mallarmés Cat

On a cold, rainy, February night in New York, I remembered the story André Malraux used to tell – and which, at some remove, was told to me – about Mallarmé's cat, whose name, almost needless to say, was Blanche.

On a cold, rainy, February night in Paris, a thin and bedraggled alley cat, wandering the streets, looks in the window of Mallarmé's house and sees a white, fat, and fluffy cat dozing in an overstuffed chair by a blazing fire. He taps on the window:

"Comrade cat, how can you live in luxury and sleep so peacefully when your brothers are out here in the streets starving?"

"Have no fear, comrade," Blanche replied, "I'm only pretending to be Mallarmé's cat."

Atlantis

It was all a dream from the holothurians. The holothurians, despised by men, called "sea cucumbers" after that insipid vegetable, dismissed as cylindrical purplish blobs, nothing more than a mouth and an anus, forever filtering mud in the gloom of the ocean floor – it was the holothurians who did it. For each is the cell of a huge collective brain, a brain trapped in millions of useless bodies that inhabit the dullest stretches on earth.

To amuse itself, this brain has spun stories along its submarine network, stories that bubbled up and randomly entered the dreams of the sleeping people above. Stories that provoked strange longings for the ocean floor: that the origin of all life began there, that forgotten kingdoms lie there in the mud, along with the shipwrecks of fantastic wealth. A dream that Solon and Plato and Bacon and de Falla and the others could only partially remember: they wrote it down, then went to sleep again to recover the rest, and never could. A dream that has led so many to dive into the sea and keep swimming down.

Atlantis! In the dark the holothurians eat and excrete and move on and eat, inching forward, thinking, sending out their mental flares in the hope that someone, something, anything will drop by and relieve the tedium of their biological fate, down there, at the bottom of the sea, with the calcified sponges, magnesium nodules, the crushed spines of sea urchins, the ghosts of coelenterates, unexploded torpedoes, skeletons of bathypterids and halosaurs, the hieroglyphic tracks of sea pens and ophiuroids, fecal coils, the waving arms of a burrowed brittle-star, manganese-encrusted dolphin teeth, the remains of a jettisoned crate of manilla-envelope clasps, zeolite crystals, pillows of basalt, calcareous shells of pteropods, the sinister egg-casings of skates, the broken anti-matter locks from a crashed spaceship, the short-crested ripples of sand and the scour moats forming in globigerina ooze.

The Sahara

Camels' feet leave lotus-pad prints
in the sand.

The Mara

The Mara, in northeast India, say that ordinary mortals, when they die, go to Athiki, the village of the dead. There it is night when it is day here, and day when it is night. Fish are bamboo leaves there, and bears are hairy caterpillars. The spirit lives for a long time in Athiki, but ultimately dies and comes back to earth. The spirit of a powerful person turns into a bit of heat mist that rises into the sky. The spirit of a poor person becomes a worm and is eaten by a chicken.

They say that when people dream, their souls wander off at the end of a long invisible string. When they have a bad dream, they tell everyone about it. When they have a good dream, they keep it to themselves.

They say that there is a giant ficus tree growing on the moon, and the marks on the moon's face that we see are its branches. Living in the tree is a headless monkey.

The greatest hunters go forever to paradise, called Peira. It is close to the one God and occupied by few, for one must have killed a man in battle, an elephant, a tiger, a bear, a small tree bear, a serow, a gural, a mithun, a rhinoceros, a sambhur, a barking deer, a wild boar, a crocodile, a hamadryad, an eagle, one of each of the kinds of hornbill, and a king crow. Government troops now keep the peace, and many of the animals are no longer there, so it is unlikely that any Mara will ever go to paradise again.